For Jim

long promised...
A small token of
my appreciation
of you

xox
Mariza*
March 30 '94

as in
" Poem in Four
Movements for
my Sister ____ "
p.63.

Memoir

by Honor Moore

Mourning Pictures (play)

The New Women's Theatre: Ten Plays by Contemporary American Women (editor)

Memoir

Poems by

Honor Moore

Chicory Blue Press   Goshen, Connecticut

Chicory Blue Press, Goshen, Connecticut 06756
© 1988 by Honor Moore. All rights reserved.
Printed in the United States of America

Book Designer: Virginia Anstett

Typeface: ITC New Baskerville. Printed on Mohawk Vellum
acid-free paper.

This book was edited, designed and typeset using Macintosh
computers. Quark XPress was used for page make-up.

Typesetting was done on a Linotronic 300 by Hoblitzelle
Graphics, North Haven, Connecticut.

Printed by Eastern Press, New Haven, Connecticut.

Cover photograph, *Bryonia alba*, by Karl Blossfeldt is
reproduced courtesy of Ann and Jürgen Wilde.

The photograph of Honor Moore is reproduced courtesy
of Inge Morath.

Library of Congress Cataloging-in-Publication Data
Moore, Honor, 1945-
    Memoir : poems.

    I. Title.
PS3563.O617M66   1988   811'.54   88-25647
ISBN 0-9619111-1-5 (pbk.)

To my father

Some of these poems first appeared in *American Review, Black Box, Chrysalis, Feminist Studies, Iowa Review, The Litchfield County Times, Maenad, The Nation, New England Review/Bread Loaf Quarterly, The New Republic, New Virginia Review, New West, Shenandoah, Sojourner, Thirteenth Moon, The Volunteer, Woman Poet: The East,* and *Yellow Silk.*

Spuyten Duyvil first appeared in *The Village Voice,* June 15, 1982.

.   .   .

I would like to thank the National Endowment for the Arts for a Creative Writing Fellowship which partially supported the writing of this book, the MacDowell Colony where some of these poems were written, and the editors, friends and poets who, affirming or criticizing, have inspired me to greater depth and clarity.

I am grateful to Sondra Zeidenstein and Virginia Anstett of Chicory Blue Press for bringing *Memoir* into the world with grace and care; to my agent, Wendy Weil, for her endurance; and to Moira Kelly whose questions and ideas unsettle and invigorate.

H.M.

Contents

I.

Spuyten Duyvil

The bridge between the Bronx and Manhattan crosses a small body of water which runs between the Hudson and the East River and is called Spuyten Duyvil, Dutch for "the devil's tail."

1.

A computer chip malfunctions. A micro-
scopic switch slips. You cut an apple into

quarters. East of the Urals, a technician
sweats into gray fatigues. In Nevada

a video screen registers activity.
The President carries a briefcase called

the football. His men sit at a small table
or cluster in easy chairs watching a screen

tick with revelation. You adjust your
blinds. I flip a cellar switch. A terrorist

monitors the football. A red light on a red
telephone flashes. The technician cues

his superior. Afternoon in the desert.
Dead of night in the Urals. Rockets

surge from concrete silos like lipsticks sprung
from gargantuan tubes. I have seen bridges

dynamited in 3-D color, mushroom clouds
engorge and shrivel in 4/4 time, faces

of children etched with acid to rippling
wound on screens the size of footballs.

So have you. In a cellar where the ceiling is
low, I bump my head, shatter the only source

of light. This cellar was not built airtight,
but I keep firewood here, my water pump, boiler.

2.

I am driving across the bridge
which connects the Bronx to

Manhattan, river blue below, sun
rippling its surprising expanse

and always entering New York
by this route, I love life.

Planes. No, missiles. Or must we
call them warheads? How fast?

Morning: You stand at your kitchen
telephone then drive down the hill.

Or twilight: You bend at a keyboard
moving as you play. Ten minutes

from that place to this. Frozen
expression on the face of

the drunk who wipes my windshield
on the Bowery. I want your

hand. Warheads. You slip an apple,
quarter by quarter, into your mouth.

We never sat facing each other:
What might we make of this love?

3.

Anyone who calls a broken heart
a metaphor hasn't seen the crack

in this sunset, fire clouds parting,
cylindrical beasts roaring

toward us. Do they land? Or do objects
tumble blazing, each from an open

hatch? Sudden light so bright
it brings utter darkness. Sound so loud

it could be silence. I am blind and
I step from my car. My hair is

on fire. It could be an earring
or an orange pinwheel. My hand is

burning. My hair stinks when it
burns. Below this bridge at the tip of

the city is a white sand beach. Did you
know that? Tell me, why don't you

reach for my hand? We are all blind, all
feel heat which mounts so fast

I can't tell if I sweat or shiver.

4.

My hair has burned back to my
scalp and now my skin is

burning off my brain. Flesh melts
down my leg like syrup. We

won't walk to the river. There's
no mirror and my head is too hot

to touch. The birds are
burning. They say cities will melt

like fat. That one has fewer bones.
Breathe? He was just collecting

our quarters. We were dancing. They
told me this would happen:

Hot oceans, flat darkness.
I stay awake to speak this:

My fingers have burned to bone and so
have yours. I never wanted a child,

but I saved everything important
so those who came after could learn.

5.

It has not been explained to us that
a computer chip has the shape of

a wafer but is invisible to the
naked eye or that a switch has less

thickness than a capillary or that
the cloud of fire is as fierce and huge as

Niagara Falls. You have chosen
this distance: We will not hear

the terrible news together. When they
tell us we have the power to stop this,

we speak only of our powerlessness
to stop a blizzard in April. There is

nothing more I could have said to you.
You cross the Golden Gate. Planes?

No, missiles. How fast? None of the
children believe they will be

grandparents. Those behind bars will burn
behind bars and I think of flowers. Why

doesn't this scare me as much as losing
love again or not having enough

money? I will break a bone or my bones
will burn. I can't see what's happening

in Nevada. I keep giving them money.
You're not here. My breath

is burning. We must go downstairs, take
hands with the others, speak something.

6.

When they said put your head to the wall,
fold your arms behind your neck, I was

not afraid. Even when I saw the movies,
I wasn't afraid, but I am afraid of

burning, of burning and breaking. When
they say we will burn, I feel knives. When

they say buildings will fly apart, that
I will be crushed by a concrete buttress or

a steel beam, I hear the weeping of
everyone into whose eyes I have been

afraid to look. If men carried knives
in airplanes, this is how it would be:

Airplanes are silver. They fly across the sky
which is blue. One day a hatch falls open,

knives fly down like rain, and we are all cut
and all bleed. What if, day after day,

knives fell from the sky? I would go into my
cellar, hope my roof would repel knives.

Failure of love has brought us to this.

7.

You iron. It could be thunder. They keep
listening to music. Let me tell you, the

difference is the whole city is an
oven which won't go out, and if it could

there would be no one to put it out.
Let me tell you, you will never

see morning again or early spring. Look,
fire sheets down the river like wind

before a hurricane. Listen, it rushes
through city streets like falls down a mountain.

No one will read what you write. No one will
eat what you put on the table. It is not

thunder. There is no time to make amends.
You will not know her as you wished,

and you will never see your face in the
faces of your nieces and nephews.

8.

Peel the apple with a knife.
Eat the apple without peeling it.

Choose beautiful paper to draw
her head or draw it on a napkin

after dinner. Eat eggs and sausage
and oranges for breakfast

or don't eat. Drink tea or drink
coffee. Call your father to wish him

happy birthday. Use a bandaid when
you scratch your hand on rose thorn, or

bleed freely into your grandmother's
linen. Plant potatoes as you planned.

Let the candles burn down to stumps
or replace them with new ones.

I have wanted to be free to feel,
to welcome you with flowers,

see your smile time after time.
When the apple limb fell, too heavy

with rain and fruit, I painted its wound
with tar. This year I will fertilize

14

so the tomatoes have no hardship.
I am not afraid to begin to love or

to keep loving. Even in this fire,
it is not fear I feel but heartbreak.

9.

Because he is afraid and powerful
he lives encircled by water.

We hold her as she dies, turn the chairs
to face each other. We breathe with her

as her child is born, let him
cry in the dark as he mourns her death.

When we don't have what we need,
we use what is nearest. One day he

swims the moat to explore the place
which confuses him. There is food when

he reaches the lit house, and stars
hang from the towering branches

of ancient trees. We must learn to rest
when we are tired. Every morning

the sun rises. Every spring green
returns to the cold climates. Bathe

with her, stand with her in her house
smiling as she shows you the

new wood. If their anger frightens you,
try to understand their grief. If you can't

understand what they say, watch
how they move. It's thunder. She

is young. Tell her the truth. He is near
ninety. Help him cross the street. It's

thunder. Reach for my hand, I will
let you go. It's raining. If you

visit, we will walk down through the fields
and I will show you the river.

II.

Cut Outs

Since we do this on the telephone, you don't
see the daily face, cereal, fresh juice,
my eyes when you cut out leaving your voice
behind, the falling child whose breath won't
come. When I come to, I have become want
the color of those snipped triangles loose
on the floor after they cut out the house
and two big figures. The depth of the want,
they keep saying, is from the past: hot
oatmeal, a pitcher of cream from the cows
nuzzling in that oval cut from silver,
juice blazing orange, a child's cries not
heeded. But this is the present: How
to stay close, up against that old scissor.

Portrait of Manet's Wife

his painting of Suzanne Leenhoff (Mrs. Edouard Manet)
in the Metropolitan Museum of Art

He kept scraping the paint from the canvas.
After all those years of looking, he simply
couldn't see her face

clearly, and so he abandoned the work,
leaving it in its present incomplete
state. Yet what is clear

is the feeling, the almost cavernous
passion his blear of stripped canvas catches,
suspends for us, which

is how my stippled memory holds, then
blanks you. It is perhaps a consequence
of love I can't hold

all of you in one frame of remembering.
Each memory scrapes another free
so that all I feel

undulates beneath an image of you
which changes as if you, not memory,
had consequences

of color and light. Or perhaps he'd lost
the love which could move his imagination
to complete her, and

could not find in the play of memory
a face as true as the naked nubble his
scalpel left three times.

In *Mrs. N's Palace*

Louise Nevelson retrospective
Whitney Museum, 1980

An hour I waited for you. And her. Gold. Black. *First*
    Personage. Shreds of what would happen here
        would piece with how we had loved,
     altering it. Waited. Black boxes, black
finials screwed to buttons and knobs, naked spools,
        gold fluted columns. Waited
     until you came, until there were three to walk
     the black rooms. *Night Presence, Cascade,* feeling you
all mine: *Dawn's Wedding,* white air as I kiss and kiss. Now
     her presence: lids pulled from barrels, tops without
        baskets, black hooks lifted, poised,
     painted to the sides of so many black boxes –
nothing to fasten. You loved her first. Shapes tilt. Harsh
     ripple of washboard white makes serene. Red
     silk blouse, light in the room like moon. Slats
        cut from wood pleat until
they drape. We could have been serene. You move to her, your
     face toward me. I wore red to stand out. In gold,
        whispering, you repeat I
     want you; in black, I want her. Spools, finials,
chaos flattened with paint. You shimmering in profile,
        she at an angle, looking.
     It looks like a breastplate. If it weren't
     art, I could take it, wear it. Black boxes stacked,
teeth on a stem. Buttons. Brushes. All this in boxes
     held. Hold. Out of black to free standing
        black on white so black looks saw-
     tooth sharp. Hold me. Edges. Is it light spilling
or are we crying? Wood feather-shaped, swirl of tools screwed
     static, black. Knob without a door. I show you
     black reeds bending from barrels, a knob shaped like
        your breast. *Royal Tide.* No door

to prepare us. *Moon Garden*. We've come this far. Bend
   with me, loosen your shoes. Let your feet fall
   with mine, naked to the black mirror floor.

Poem for the Beginning

Noon, the sky gray, the snow not falling in earnest, so
the day seems odd, too usual, almost boring, the light
     from the slight new cover on the old snow not
broken, played by the sun with color, but flat, intensely
          white. This morning, a woman was saying,
               separation is good for
     love. She has been here a month, I two days, and
this new snow on old ice is slippery: I have fallen
twice. Weeks ago, I said, I want to be only happy
     with you, and you said, there are always other
feelings. What I mean is, I want to care for you, care as
          for the most delicate plant or creature, care
               as one guards a singular
     gift which is fragile, beautiful. Last night
by telephone, we tried to arrange your visit. You
couldn't say, definitely yes, because a nearly past
     love will visit, you must see her, so you
cannot tell me yes, definitely, this day, because
          she has not said definitely, yes, that
               day. Last night on a pay phone,
     we talked an hour, bare bulb dangling, giving
light, I tracing my returned dime with purple ball point,
moving the dime, drawing in its circle first a face,
     then hair. I don't trust what happens when you
see her, I say, scribble out eyes, mouth, move the dime, trace
          another. I'm feeling what might be my
               love for you like a change in
     temperature, wondering if I must be unsure
to feel it. This circle stays hollow. I scratch out from
its edge – flames, as if a purple sun were eclipsed by a white
          dime moon. I wish she'd disappear, I say, and

regret it. Let's not talk about her, you say, your hair
       flooding my mind like coal-colored water,
           black rushing from thick ice
   on the river in town, black tongue flooding from
white lips which thaw and refreeze. I want to be only
happy with you, not held back. I want to care for you as
      for a delicate plant. I want you to care
for me. A woman near the fire says, I have found love
       this way between women: a see-saw, one up,
          the other – Care for you as
   I want to hold you, my legs firm, your body
resisting their force. Care as I want my mouth moving
against yours, as it does, as it has against no one else's
      mouth. Care as I want to lie beside you, our
faces close, look into you, dark, through your cordovan
      eyes. *Separation is good for – This way –*
        A see-saw – Jealousy and
    possession, the woman says, are our least
legitimized feelings. And you to care for me. This
day, light stays the same, trees don't move: silence, then an
      occasional creak, the oil burner
roaring, measuring time by cold and heat – on, off, on.
      A six-pronged shell, gift from you, balances
         on its transparent stand, seems
   to float, image of heat, pink center of heat
burning out, still and continuing, as if the hot
color of a daylily opening were heat rather
      than color. This cold between us is distance,
circumstance. Just how, I ask her, is separation good?
     Going away, she says, coming back – almost
       waving her hand as she speaks –
I like coming back, leaving and coming back. Coming back.

Hotel Breakfast

"I want no sexual –" announces he
in turquoise, shirt wrinkling
across his chest, "– involvement." My
toast had popped up. I was watching

the sun on the snow reach
eight o'clock. "It's just as beauti-
ful here in spring," someone says, "or
summer." I am buttering when

my egg arrives poached, pure on bone
china. I eat it watching him
intently spoon down oatmeal, his
turquoise collar, his erotic

neck. I am trying to watch the
sun reach eight-fifteen. I resist
a pumpernickel bagel. I
am trying not to watch

the turquoise move tight against his
"Coffee?" "Russia," someone starts,
"will never be a normal
country, because it never has…"

Premonition

Brink of September. Mountains rise as I drive.
I enter where they are highest, where clear springs
wash trunks of spruce, where white everlastings
splash dusk-dark meadows, where north means wild.

Lake ringed with mountains. I shout, hear it back,
back. I do not imagine in days I will
touch your face, trace with my fingers what it has
lived without me. I shampoo, dive to rinse.

Labor Day. I gather tomatoes, twist ripe
zucchini from ridged vines, pluck lettuce, crush
basil for your return. I hike home through birch
carrying new caught trout. At the slide I strip.

Sun heats bright moss. Brook foams fast through cleft
concrete. I sit, let it rush me wet down smooth
rock to a pool clean of twigs. Cold water whirls
to my skin, quick as the breath of fresh passion.

Poem for the End

You leave. I write what happened, type it – onion skin. A romance
      you called it. Save carbons, airmail it: love letter to
         a married man. A year later, standing
      where you and I stood, a woman talks –
         execution of Basques in Spain,
a photographer who'd seen it, whom she interviewed.
      She leaves him, changes her mind, goes back. "We made
         love –" she talks fast. "We can't give up, must find ways

to nurture men, not lose autonomy –" Alone I've come back
      to heal. Tsvetaeva writes a poem: Death and the loss
         of love, her blond captain, are
      interchangeable. All day, as if waiting, I
         play records, Beethoven again
and again. A novel of passion. A triangle:
      three women. Intense pain about this thwarted love, writes
         a critic, marks the start of her mature

vision. As if to live completely, one must lose love. As if
      to gain knowledge one must lose the first romance, a blond
         captain. Last night, because of the music,
      in the dark, my own hands, I touched delicately
         the place between, opening my
thighs, touched as if you, as if filling one's own need were –
      as if easy. Use anger. What has had to be
         translated. Talk about the craziness of

trying to write the ultimate. Music. A sense of place. And
        it rains. Snow sinks inches a day even in sun. I
                still don't have a color photograph: how
            the sun sets here, which colors the snow reflects, and
                the snow is melting. In a room
across the road, the man I wait for sits with another
        woman. I am waiting as if for a lover
                for a man not my lover. I wait for him

as if he knows I wait, as if for my lover for this
        man I have decided not to love because I love
                someone else. Wait through fatigue for the poem
            about you, feeling, like nausea, the craziness,
                my anger. Not at. From. Last night
this: a man – fantasy – comes to my bed. I love him
        as no one else has, mouth him until his eyes half-
                close, till he cannot speak, until he rocks. "We

fucked our brains out," she says. "Makes you understand why men want
        those encounters – short – that freedom." If I were a painter
                working the small area near my mouth:
            In one year this face has learned her most powerful
                emotion is powerless. There's
something new in her. I would want you to know it
        by the mouth. Alone I've come back to this place. This
                is not my normal state. I am a person

with friends. I live in a context. I do not wait for men. I
    do not wait, without interruption, for poems. There is
        someone I love. I rarely work after
          dinner, maybe twice a year. Once I flew to France to
           meet a married man. Just once, for
love. Passion: let a whole moment move through you without
    the fear of being cruel. That's the balance, a perfect
        sunny July day. The actual is

fitful and relentless as March, a final thaw. Often
    passion has had to be translated. "We stood against
        the glass, touching it, watching the late sun
        on the East River, acknowledging its beauty,
          then we made love." But what did you
say that he knew what you wanted? "You don't have to say
    anything." The perfect sunny day. Did you think love
        was a chat at a small table? Was it love

last night, that hand, unexpected, through my hair? Can love be
    a telephone call in which a voice you love, long
        distance, tells you not to be afraid as
        you wait for the poem? Or is love just want. Last night
        I wanted someone. Alone in
a dark room, radio, a piano pure as black
    Eurydice's wild dance, shocking as a full white
        rose, cooling as water, sweet as love or hands

touching that delicate place, scent of hyacinth. I wanted
so much, wanted someone to want, to come to me wanting
me. Winter, just a year ago, you, whom
I loved, were leaving. Perhaps we would never see
each other again that way, that
passionately, yet we prepare as if we are to
leave together, I driving through sunset, night, to the
train. Kissing, you say "I've never understood

kissing at trains," then swiftly, "Goodbye, better this way" – and choose
a seat behind the only fogged window. The night is
intensely cold, the moon a harsh orange
sickle rocking on its back. I have not seen him
that way again. A voice. A hand
through hair. Such wounds do not heal quickly. Do you think love
is just a chat at a table? Was it love he looked at
me with? If I were a painter, I would

work the area near the mouth for days. This woman knows now
you have some things fleetingly, that's all. Would you know that
by her mouth? I soothe myself. Honey.
Hibiscus. And music. An airport terrace at
Nice. I wait to leave the same man,
frightened I'll miss my flight. He doesn't – won't – speak. I want
him to say I love you. He won't. Didn't. A woman,
a stranger, walks toward us, dyed red hair, breasts

heavy, jouncing against a lime green sweater. "Oooh la la! Oooh
la la, Madame!" This out loud, say you whom I love, not
in jest, to a woman, a stranger, and
I leave in minutes. You kiss me, just lightly. We
certainly will, perhaps never
see one another again. Across the road, a room,
light. A man sits with another woman. I depend
on music written by a deaf man dead

two hundred years for sustenance, to get beyond my too
strong sense of place. What has had to be translated does
not translate back into one language. I
wait, with Beethoven. Some fear is gone, you can tell
in my voice, the poem pasted, three
sheets, white on the wall. I am trying to learn the
ultimate, and it shows near my mouth. There is no
photograph, how the sun sets, which colors the snow

repeats. These carbons repeat what happened between us before
you left on that train, try, while lying, to tell truth of
feeling, the truth of a moment, but
dodge facts: marriages, desire. A romance, you
called it. Use anger. Love was
translated. If you were a painter, you might have known it
in my face. At night, a year later, snow extends
this room's light. Future. This out loud: The future.

Cleis

She was young. The jeep was yellow. She
cruised past; her style was studied – a white
shirt crisply collared: a visitation, or
an extrapolation, from Sappho's
grove. Invitations had prevented our day
in bed, and we were suffering. Flowers, sun –

we had left brunch. A young woman in a sun
chariot, eyes burning beneath blond bangs, she
drove slowly toward us, a clean car. "Good day,"
she said. You noted the greeting. The white
pelargonium were still in bloom. Sappho's
girls would be weaving them into garlands, or

dancing, singing what the scent inspired, or
quilling lyres. She leaned out the window, sun
glinting off her tousled brow. Sappho
would have applauded her approach, how she
directed her gaze without guile, whites
of her eyes cosseting blue irises. "Good day"

was perhaps not all she said. It was Sunday
in California, weather like paradise or
Lesbos, clouds seductively adrift, white
as if to reassert cloud, reflecting sun-
light. Our music had begun, our swoon, when she
drove down the hill and hovered. Was she Sappho's

gold-dressed daughter Cleis? Or Sappho's
dapple-throned Aphrodite, girl for a day,
oaring down from heaven in a gold car? She
slowed nonetheless, as if she expected us, or
had somehow conjured us. We wore sun-
glasses, so she was not an attack of white

blindness, of any blindness. She was a white-
kirtled vision to tease us back to Sappho's –
dare I speak it? – bower: a trenchant, sun-
drenched mirage to accentuate a day
we were taken transcendentally, or
at least fervently, with one another. She

accelerated. White wheels whirled into day,
and, as Sappho's jeep, emblazoned NO NUKES OR
WIFE ABUSE, flashed in the sun and vanished, so did she.

35

Birthday

for Margie, February 7, 1987

Snow shoulders narrow a night road – forty
inches? twenty feet? – how high I can't
know in the dark, south of therapy
on U.S. 7. In California
it's seventy-five, though TV says perhaps
rains will bring a cool-down. As I climb

to bed, you, out to movie or meeting, climb
into "Space Blimp," speed off. When my forty
winks are up, you're dreaming deep, perhaps
a dive down sun flung coral, I can't
know. My snow-bound road's not California
but Connecticut, home from therapy

where, of course, I've mentioned you. Therapy's
no word for poems, lyric for songs which climb
inverted fifths, but to California's
women I'd write forty poems, and forty
more to its sunset weather (how you can't
see for fog some dusks on the Bay), then perhaps

I'd write a poem to you. Some, perhaps,
might say, *Again?* But we're not therapy,
we're birthday: Your birthday! So friends can't
pull armadillos from too many hats, climb
poems up too many mountains, and forty
days can't contain their bliss: California's

where we celebrate. California
where you were daughter-born; where years, perhaps
months, weeks, or just days short of forty
years back – to learn exactly, ask therapy –
but *early*, hair curling, ears perked, you climb
Mom's feet beneath the grand: No one says can't.

When you mount the bench, no one says can't
either, then fingers lick keys, California
wild flowers shiver, and roses climb
higher in your grandmother's garden. Perhaps
they climb there still, up through therapy
toward the simple difficulty of forty,

where *can't* is an old idea, *perhaps*
is *yes*, California shines like therapy,
and you climb on – Artist. Beauty. Forty.

Shenandoah

Photograph: Breakfast after our first full night:
Elbow on the table, fist against your face, intent
   on the cup you look into. Your hair glints
      in three-year-old light.
In these rooms of borrowed furniture, white
walls, wide windows that curve, I have been solitary.
   A cymbedium orchid. Artichokes. Fresh
      trout. I tear pink netting from
the orchid, float it. Red wine is breathing. A plane
lands hours away, and I can think of you driving
   a valley roofed with clouds, your voice
      like the charge of new weather.

Yesterday, eyes shut, sun on my face, I could
remember you viscerally: Heat, sun that caressed
   our naked skin, blond grasses, weeds baked
      to vivid rust. There was no
snow – odd that far north in late October. From ours
other mountains were feathery with bare trees
   and some phenomenon of light turned
      their billowing crests
lavender. See those mountains make a giant sprawled
on her back: those, breasts; the one called Otter, torso.
   See the lake bright near her cheek, the
      trout stream etch her chin.

I am afraid in the vestibule, your face
smiling its guileless welcome. I want to cry, hold you,
   open through your breasts into safe billowing
         darkness. I kiss you
as if we are just friends. I lead you through
white rooms. I hand you the orchid because I cannot
   tell you. You reach. I start, as if your touch were
         too much light. I trim
the artichokes. The red wine breathes. I must cover
the curved windows. In this valley roofed with clouds, I live
   alone in rooms on a street where
         all the shades are pulled.

We drink red wine. We unbutton, touch. We eat
trout – clouded eye, clear black night shut from the house, petal
   flush of your skin. We eat artichokes, mark
         leaf after leaf with our teeth.
The orchid floats. It is your darkness I want with my
mouth. If I could speak as sound not edged into
   word, I could tell you. Leaves now: two, four,
         five at once. We reach
center, loose lavender-streaked swirl, split the naked
heart in the night bed where I speak with my hands
   and we breathe, mouth to mouth, unedged,
         shorn to simple tenderness.

Letter in Late July

for M.

Dearest, I have resisted these, my first lines
in more than a year, waiting for you to pass
like a mood or a winter, but you persist –
a landscape. It's green,

that limpid pre-dusk hesitation at the
swell of New England summer, and I'm bereft.
The surge of comfort has thinned to a whisper:
I'm on my own

to ride the surprises: tears fast as fresh
blood: poems I wrote you two years ago appear
in the mail cold and published: I have no
address for you, or

phone. A horse, solitary, walks from a barn
against a sky white with near-night. A fawn
picks her way across a darkening road, pulls you
up out of me. You'd

be surprised, wouldn't you, to hear that tonight
I wept with frustration at no message from
a man I keep dreaming of: I'd leave women,
so eager am I

not to remind my heart of you. My roses
throb clear colors as night falls; a bird call cuts
the warm silence like a quick ax. Rebecca
looked me in the eye

40

today. You've done it, she said; you've got yourself
back. I nodded to her, post office tears still
blearing, contact lenses salt-fogged. Whatever
I might say is as

high school quaint as sobs at a mute answering
box. I quiz myself as if an answer could
alter my feelings as deftly as touching
a key reconciles

green words on a black screen. But nothing merges
painlessly enough with my memory. I
could cook a lambchop or murder mosquitoes.
I could go out or

hang out my towels. Set phrases rise to soothe me –
This too shall pass – and do, as does the sound of
the brook, of summer traffic on the road. White
mullions edge black glass;

it's night. *Broken hearts are nothing new.* It's past
three months. When I dream you, it's a haze, colors
that seem familiar. When it rains, I can hear
your voice say *listen.*

A Green Place

"What's beyond making love?" A true question.
"Time," I quip, knowing my imagining
 seeks an answer to soothe fear from your face. If
we could freeze the instant in sex when light
shudders and we let time go, the clear
light of morning which turns lush green

 silvery. Beyond making love? Green
if it's a place. Here any question
leads to an answer if put clearly,
 here all responsive gestures feed imagining
and nature has no difficulty. Light
of noon: We are making love as if

 it is a path. I am kissing you as if
what I drink from you is a river through green
breath, as if you are a source of light,
 as if the feel of your mouth rendered questions
obsolete, as if simple imagining
extended vision without exacting a clear

 equivalent in risk. Beyond this? Clear
dark of evening shadows your face. If
we lived as though time were, like imagining,
an easy skittering, an ascent through green
familiarity till colors, like questions,
need no assured compliment, then light,

freed of its debt to time, could make light
of fear, leave just what grief makes clear –
smooth pebbles in a crystal bowl. But questions
like yours darken like night or storm. What if
I can't answer? I see you in a green
place looking at me, but my imagining

doesn't speak in answers. Imagining
is formed in a slow rush of memory: light,
fear, sound, weather. Ecstatic smell of new green,
touch of a lover's skin, cheek, mouth. Clear
liquid glinting in sunlight dazzle. If
you insist I answer, the question

is lost to your imagining. If I claim clear
knowledge, light that loosens memory darkens. If
love's beyond love, it's green. We share the question.

III.

Dream

*after hearing Adrienne Rich lecture on
Emily Dickinson*

Your eyes are smudges on a moon face.
You pack for a trip. The room of rags

you pull into order is dark. I stand
at a distance. Your mother,

old, sits beyond you, arms
folded, chest broad like yours, hair to

head like yours, but ash. She moves,
a primate, rhythmically picking,

throwing. She knows this labyrinth –
which rag, which broken object to pack

in which tattered box.
Suddenly she moans: No words,

but the meaning breaks a darkness inside me
and I cry with my whole body.

I move closer, see your face
focus, dissolve to your

mother's face: her face, your face,
hers, yours, hers, until you merge,

say to me, I will not go away.

Legacies

White envelope addressed to your mother in red ink – your
   hand; my journal reread after five years: *I hope*
      she doesn't die; a Wanda Landowska
     record pulled from a dusty shelf – I play her
playing as you did, Bach over and over, when I was
   a child; young composer, jazz singer mother ten years
     dead, stands with me in a cellar, smokes,
waits for laundry: "Just before she died," he says, "my mother
   said, if you become a musician, I want you to
     stand someday on a stage, sing this." He turns
    his back, sings, *When there are gray clouds, I don't mind*
the gray clouds, I'm all for you sonny boy, all for you. Mom,
   I miss you and he tells me it doesn't go away.
     Mom, last winter in this room I cried
in a man's arms, my willingness to love stretching to
   reach someone alive: It was as if I could see my
     heart below me, dark, a mountain range watched
    from a cruising jet. I was crying and I saw death
move out of me, swiftly, like the massed shadows of clouds,
   black, seen from the sky on a clear day, recede, leaving
     just sunlight. Mom: your music, her hands, the
keys moving, live, forceful, speaking – the harpsichord – prelude,
   fugue, prelude – past death. Mom, after five years I believe
     and can't believe you died. Last night, the wind,
    a window opening: "Mom," I shout, half-joke,
"Mom!" remembering the strong strange wind in the huge maples
   the night they called to say you'd gone into a coma.
     Tomorrow you're fifty-five. Mom, I'm

thirty-two, and the you that lives on in me sometimes
is not enough. Mom, I wear my hair pulled back with combs.
Mom, I keep my room neat, exercise. Mom,
I ride a horse once a week and keep seeing
you take Grandma's bay mare through that course of jumps: Over and
over: I am a child, the horse throws you. In that dusk
I begin to learn what it might be
to lose you, but always you walk back, stride back, embarrassed,
glasses broken, wet from your fall in the evening
grass, no gray in your black hair. Mom, when I
visited your grave in the snow and could not
move from the hillside because in the cold I saw your mouth
pinken to its living color and smile at me, Mom,
was that real? I sit in this room,
orange curtains billowing in the light – flowers, basket,
star stitched through the Amish quilt – magenta, green, blue – your
colors, and the dead woman plays as if
alive, moving her long hands, making a deep
sinewy river of each delicate baroque line: Mom,
I am thirty-two. The you that lives on in me is
sometimes not enough. You died before
your mother. You can't know what it is not to have one. There's
snow on the ground here as there was in Massachusetts
the day they buried Grandma. Months after
you died, she told this dream: a place with snow, she
thinks Canada. You are dead but alive, and she rocks you,
rocks you, and you forgive her. Mom, does she rock you now
or do you rock her? At the funeral

the priest said, our sister enters the gates of paradise
in a company of angels. Mom, were you waiting?
I have no mother, your mother's gone, and
the you that lives on, me, I must learn she is
enough. From this room I see snow. Snow. Tomorrow is your
birthday. This is for you. The snow is melting. I've built
a fire. Mom, the fingers of the dead
woman play as if in some paradise, paradise, and
your mouth pinkens to breathing red and smiles. I am here,
your daughter, wanting. *When there are gray
clouds, I don't mind the gray clouds. I'm all for you.* All from you.

Sitting for Inge Morath

Her camera – then a focused face
maneuvers to seek with a blue eye
what in my face she would embrace.

"I have an idea," her smile a trace
to reassure – and posing, I comply.
Her camera, then a focused face

catch a countenance I'd efface.
She's triumphant, almost wry.
What in my face she would embrace

I can't predict. We talk of place,
become friends, light moves with each try:
Her camera, then a focused face

(together a sort of minotaur) race
shadow and my poise to prophesy
what in my face she would embrace

in darkroom darkness, how I'll grace
paper – first a fray of shadow filched by
her camera, then a focused face:
what in my face she would embrace.

In the Circus, 1905

photograph by Harry C. Rubincam

Until now I've danced the tightrope, spun
the high trapeze. Today, "Do it on horseback."
Mr. Harry hoods himself. It's his black
snout that frightens me, not the Lippizan.
I stand, heels rooted to her slick white skin,
my feet in third. It's later on the rope
I want his flash to catch my balance – soaped
shoes, ostrich plume mask – not now. Children
hush. The tent glows like Mama's seashell torch.
I curve my arms high: horse is ocean, earth –
Flashpowder. Noise. Hold as she breaks? Not a chance.
Fixed in his dark rinse, I ride again. Etched,
a *port de bras* on glass, I rise, a birth,
to his occasion, balance. My last dance.

To Janet, On *Galileo*

Bertolt Brecht's Galileo
Havermeyer Hall at Columbia, 1978

In the play about the first telescope, a man notes
    through Galileo's strange tube a moon's edge
not precise or sharp, but irregular, serrated.

    We face each other, two women friends, a small
table. Mouth ached to a smile, you begin: *The balance –*
    job, marriage, writing – it's stopped working. Passion

of discovery: Brecht argues such passion is true
    reason. You contemplate leaving a man. I
have left a man. A Hungarian restaurant. Sun

    not earth is center. Galileo argues
Copernicus. Priests argue heaven, Ptolemy,
    crystal spheres that never move, refuse to look

through the telescope. A man weeping. I cannot touch
    him. To comfort would keep me here. You speak of
leaving, feel abandoned. Fork lifted: *Perhaps I am*

    insatiable. Perhaps no one can love me
enough. Chicken paprikash, red cabbage, red wine. Gold
    light of April evening. Young women, young arms

wreathing young men, whisper near university walls.
    Janet, women like us are caught in history,
a diaspora. A Leonard Woolf taking care is

    not enough. We are not willing to forfeit
passion of love to have passion of work: We want both.
    A man's blunt body on blue sheets. Sweetness of

years. I leave, go on more alone. *Yesterday we talked*
until night. Maybe it's time to part, is what
we came to. Janet, when I knew I had to leave the

house where we'd lived seven years, I cried every
morning. If there were a child, perhaps I could not have
left. Unrestricted inquiry, they warn him,

is dangerous for mankind. Galileo, obsessed,
keeps eye to glass, night, Jupiter's four moons, hears
no warning. *If I leave, will anyone else ever*

love me? Janet, I was in bed with my new
love kissing when I saw us: sweet Sunday, him, me
seven years younger walking near the blue

river way downtown. Late lunch in a bar, blue sky fall
vivid. I couldn't stop crying until I
reached the telephone, called. I don't know if I cried for

the loss of him, for the loss of a me who
could live with him, or for the loss of what I didn't
know we'd lost until that night I walked through snow

with someone else. Ice air came in me like freezing breath,
stars bristled a black sky, my mind knew I must
get out. A student in the presence of his mentor:

Galileo, old, blind, silenced. The young man
asks, "Have you truly recanted?" "Yes, I have seen their
instruments of torture, and my body fears

pain." Janet, I keep seeing a woman forty-one
        stop painting: sanatoriums, shock, drugs; her
daughter, after nine children, begins to write: cancer,

        dead at fifty. I am her daughter. Yes, my
body fears. Galileo at the telescope: Three
        moons near Jupiter! I've proved Copernicus –

heaven moves! Writes his last at night, prisoner, candle-
        lit, racing blindness. The young man smuggles it
free. Janet, we must risk our fear, this history. I say

        we must be insatiable. We walk, theatre
into cool night, moon silver in a black sky. Edge not
        serrated, but smooth. Perfect as a clear choice.

First Time: 1950

In the back bedroom, laughing when you pull
something fawn-colored from your black
tight pants, the unzipped chino slit.
I keep myself looking at the big belt
buckled right at my eyes, feel the hand
riffle my hair: You are called Mouse, baby-

sitter trusted Wednesdays with my baby
brother. With me. I still see you pull
that huge bunch of keys from a pocket, hand
them to my brother, hear squeaking out back –
Mrs. Fitz's clothesline – as you unbelt,
turn me to you, my face to the open slit.

It's your skin, this thing, head, its tiny slit
like the closed eye of a still-forming baby.
As you stroke, it stiffens like a new belt –
your face gets almost sick. I want to pull
away, but you grip my arm. I see by your black
eyes you won't let go. With your left hand

you take my chin. With your other hand
you guide it, head reddening, into my slit,
my five-year-old mouth. In the tight black
quiet of my shut eyes, I hear my baby
brother shaking the keys. You lurch, pull
at my hair. I don't breathe, feel buckle, belt,

pant. It tastes lemony, musty as a belt
after a day of sweat. Mouth hurts, my hands
push at your hips. I gag. You let me pull
free. I open my eyes, see the strange slits
yours are; you don't look at me. "Babe, babee –"
You are moaning, almost crying. The black

makes your skin clam-white now, your jewel-black
eyes blacker. You buckle up the thick belt.
When you take back the keys, my baby
brother cries. You extend a shaking hand
you make kind. In daylight through a wide slit
an open shade leaves, I see her pull,

Mrs. Fitz pulling in her rusty, soot-black
line. Framed by a slit, her window, her large hands
flash, sort belts, dresses, shirts, baby clothes.

Ruth

She deserted him. He was
career army. She was through
marching, had a baby son,
no money, was fat, jittery, bone-
tired, but her own woman.

She came up north, wore pink nights,
left the kid in a pup tent.
When Bill with the green pickup
landed in State nuts, she married shaved
bald Ben, gold ring through his nose.

They said her aunt stole the kid –
"Ben deals drugs," they said, "she's
been drinking." But I saw her cold
sober shooting skeet at the town fair
without a man, and thinner.

Younger Brother

I.

She says the fire aged you fifteen years – now
you look like that stern official photograph,
      Pop, hornrimmed, peering. I gave her my
sheepskin coat, a black velvet thirties dress.
      She had no clothes left, neither did you.
I gave her summer shoes, a mauve silk tunic
with pants. She couldn't speak or scream. Her friend
      Sharon shoved her to the window. Smoke.
Trucks. A midnight sky pink with fire lights you
      home. You find them in a squad car, mute,
huddled. Arson. You keep wearing the same two
shirts. I've been burning. Everything burned except
      a folder she took when she knew it
was fire. All your paintings, five years' work. Burning
      myself all fall in the kitchen. Pop
called that morning: you were out buying basics.
I called back to offer help. You look like me.

II.

    Because she loves you, I gave her clothes
I've held onto: a linen vest, a bright silk
    scarf – purple bled to gold like the shapes
you paint. Burning myself. Boiling water for
eggs. I spill. Steam hisses, sears. My right side. Weeks
    before the fire she moved passport and
documents from her folder to a drawer. Burns
    through pants, tights. Skin screams as if sliced, thigh
purples. How many paintings? A salmon silk
blouse I've worn since college. Sharon screaming from
    the window. At your party, paintings
tacked to a wall, the first I've seen since you were
    fifteen. Boots, tap shoes, silver pumps, her
parade of shoes. Burned. Torrents of flame. Fire-
men hosing, hatcheting. She and Sharon the
    last rescued. Your studio locked, all
your paintings. The firemen there two whole days.

III.

You've lived here a year. You've never called me. I
haven't seen you except moments at family
     occasions. Once you grabbed my arm so
it hurt. Nothing in the hot ash but bright flecks,
     plastic melted, remelted. You took
my best friend out to dinner. I couldn't ask
your phone number. When I look into your face
     nothing I recognize gleams back. I
told you I'd moved downtown. You said, maybe I'll
     run into you. Once on Eighth Street, but
no chance to talk until your party. I said
I liked the paintings. You said nothing. One
     especially. Your chalk face, nothing
answering but desert color on canvas –
     flesh, clay, cream. To weep instead, hold. If
I could hold you long enough to burn myself
through to you, weep. I am a person you love.

IV.

 A white wool jacket, the elegant
gray sweater you gave me your second Paris
  Christmas. Before Boston, years before
New York. I've been afraid to wear it, afraid
a sweater holding so much silence might burn.
  I invited you both, she came. We
sat eating breakfast in a sunny room. I
  gave her a blue striped shirt to give you. If
change could always have the speed of fire, if
I could understand what burns behind your
  changed face. The sunny room. You and I
drink the coffee, tear the bread, choose what she'd want
  from my years of clothes. All your paintings
burned, will that bring relief? I did not give her
the sweater. If hope brought what's hoped for as fire
  leaves ashes, if I wear the sweater,
if I risk the burning, can the burning stop?

Poem in Four Movements for my Sister Marian

I.
There has always been something strange about
how gracefully six-foot-two you are, something too fragile
        about your gold skin that dulls
            quick as a smile turns to a mouth
                gaping pain. In
California, between cold mountains and
a black-blue ocean, you left your college room, moved into
            a glass house I've never seen –
            "No roommates, my own space." Your first
                night alone, through
the glass in the black, a flat face, an arm
moving. Something splurts across glass, I am not there. You turn
            off the lights, see a man's bare
            legs flashing, running, disappear.
                You telephone
a boyfriend, crack open the first ice frozen
in your own house. Drink. Wait. He plays alto sax, he has
            very white teeth, not teeth blotched
            like yours, neon-white, when some drug
                cooled an infant
fever. A Mediterranean beach
burning, you flat, gold hair spread, body going dark – when your
            mother died, you took your first
            trip across an ocean – sixteen
                with a best friend:
Italy, France, Spain, Morocco – she stayed,
you blazed home. The acid North Africa sun had not bleached
            the stained front teeth, but your skin
            stayed gold for weeks. His mother is

63

dying, she has
cancer. A die-press crushed the father's arm,
he can't work. The boyfriend, twenty and very poor, can't know
what's hit him. You are trying
to teach him and stay standing, but
this cold first night
your solitude is terror shoving,
pressing in. You hear the bicycle, he bends through the door,
hands over two stolen sheets.
Together you loop a white curtain
the length of glass,
sleep. When you wake up, wrapped in each other,
you can't see the ocean, but you have forgotten the fear.

    II.

                                        Too fast.
bones through skin. Two bones break, leave
sharp points to pierce skin, skin turns
dead-white, holes bleed.
Bright sun or clouds or rain. The morning or
night, you don't say. I am not there. A truck coming, curving
down a mountain. You riding
behind a man on a motor-
cycle, your knees
sticking gracefully out. Not the one who
plays alto sax. A party, a picnic, your hair pulled back –
maybe blue on your eyelids,
a scarf swirling purple on your
neck on the way

64

to the top. I am not there. Coming down
the steep road fast, the truck slips too close to the white line, nicks
                    your left knee, breaks the leg twice –
            above the knee, and below it
                            near the ankle.
        "My knee – skin graft – conscious the whole time – I'm
all right." I put the phone receiver back in its cradle
                    a continent away. All day
                bones in my head press against
                        my brain: a dance
            class on a beach, you bending, stretching your
perfect leotard-black legs.

                    III.
            I sit next to you, watch your face,
                        avoid the leg:
            two giant casts, steel-hinged together, skin
graft exposed, oozing blood, pus. You exclaim its progress
                    like a mother. "It's March, late
            night cool, no rain yet..." you write from
                        Santa Cruz. "And
            also, I want you to trust me." A man's
cracked voice sings stereo next to your bed. I watch your face
                    mouthing his words, "I'm easy..."
            Trust you. If I were to look at
                        your knee longer
            than an instant, if I were to swab clean
the square jagged wound like the nurse does with cool cotton, if
                I touched your cast too long, if

I signed it like a high school friend,
that would mean I
accept, and it's too fast. Trust you. What if
that man that first dark night, after seeing you – blond, distant –
had come up the beach with some
blunt dark weapon, had smashed through
glass, your see-through
walls, had approached, with the weapon, you alone
in your own house. I did not see his face, can't look at yours –
the strain – as your arms lift,
guide the weighted leg carefully
to the floor, then
grasp an overhead bar and trapeze you
into the wheelchair. "Something in our relationship is
confused," you write. "And also
I want you to trust me." How
do I trust you?
You let yourself break, leaned too far and broke
like a red amaryllis pulled over by the new weight
of its huge blooms. And something
else. We sisters have been a wall,
not against, just
standing, and part fell, and the man driving
the motorcycle broke a bone that didn't need a cast
and didn't bleed. If the truck
had jumped the line completely, you
would not have lived.
What is the strength of a woman against
a truck? Against speed on a road? There has always been something

strange about how gracefully
six-foot-two you are, too graceful.
What is the strength
of a woman nineteen against dark nights
alone?

IV.
Your thick green letter resting on the window sill,
the demand, "and also, I want
you to trust me." Blood coming out
of the knee, and
pus; the dark jagged outline of the graft,
your leg shrivelled to the shape of a banister peg – you,
part of the structure of my
future, stand: image, evidence
that future is
vulnerable. "Hope you are well," you write,
"all my love." Once when I was a child clenching my hands to
fists at the movies, a drop
of sweat burned a brown stain inside
my left ring
finger. I felt the sharp point of heat, but
the mark surprised me. Yesterday, Jane, a friend not seen for
ten years, visited here from
Canada, left leg just out of
a cast. They say
she'll ski in three years, but she's a dancer –
leg smashed, a car's back fender, forty mph, two months
after yours. "The leg may be

slightly shorter," they tell you –
I am not there –
"has to wear a lift, may have a slight limp
when exhausted." Blood vessels grow back, but can a bone stretch?
If the truck had jumped the line
completely, you would not have lived.
A year later,
the neon blotches, your imperfect teeth,
the leg, you in my mind. Last winter when the amaryllis
fell and split in two, I bound
its green stalk with Scotch Magic Tape.
It grew, healed back
together – a slight lump, but from a distance
whole. And the flowers came, huge white trumpets with pink edges,
anyway. You, at a distance
whole, but more complicated than
my idea of
perfection. The mullion's shadow, a line
across the green first page of your letter. I take it from
the window sill, there is no
shadow. Jane's feet rest, in orange
sandals, on the
Oriental rug. "Does it hurt?" "I don't
know hurt anymore," she says, "but I do feel it," and pulls
her long purple skirt to her
knee. I look, want to slide my hand
along the scar
blurred through the tight surface of her stocking
but am afraid. Bones through skin, two bones break, leave sharp

points to pierce skin. You are
twenty. What you
mean by trust is letting go. How graceful
you are. Three thousand miles from here bones knit like stalks, a square
jagged scar is healing, a
chiropractor rectifies a
spine strained to the
left by the weight of two casts. You write "It
hurts less." When I see you, we will sit in the sun, your bleached
denim skirt pulled up, and
I will massage your leg, your knee,
June heat beating
down on my thirty-year-old hands, my veins
in blue relief, brown stain on a left ring finger faded.
Change. I will rub the flaccid
calf muscles, the dark scar streaks. I
will be careful
not to hurt. I will rub only the edge
of the skin graft and, shutting my eyes, see it turn lighter
as the sun turns your leg dark
leaving, imbedded in your knee
like a metal
pattern in Moroccan wood, a jagged
silver square, impervious to ultra-violet rays.

My Mother's Moustache

My mother said I'd inherit a moustache and I did.
Hers she removed with green wax she melted in a pan,
    a two inch saucepan,
        when the hairs grew too evident.
At fifteen, a dutiful daughter and fascinated
as well by my possible beauty, I bought my own
    doll-size waxworks and inherited
        my mother's ritual for a while.
I'd cook my wax, let it cool a little before spreading
it on; then I would wait for the unnatural stuff
    (this wasn't at all
        like candle-wax; it never flaked)
to harden, and eyes shut, I'd rip it all off in one piece,
relishing the hot pain, the gasping pores – ignoring
    the tears my eyes spewed against my will,
        the cowards! The first time was the worst.
My peach-fuzz moustache which I thought too bushy for beauty
was blonde and soft. Wax would not guarantee new face-hair
    as blonde or as soft.
        Even my mother said, "After
the first waxing a moustache becomes darker and thicker."
But, defying heredity and believing in
    perfectibility, I began,
        new bare-faced hopes throbbing through the pain.
It was hairless for a time. I waited, climbed on the sink
to get nearer the mirror. "Let nothing grow!" No luck.
    Sprouts pushed through my skin.
        I'd read of Russian princesses

whose lovers saw their moustaches as signs of great beauty;
now I imagined singing mezzo at La Scala,
      moustache flowing to Puccini, like
         the dark diva who smiles with Bjoerling
(Angel's long playing *La Boheme*). I stroked my new dark
hairs, vowed to keep them, and did, until pink powder turned
      my moustache orange.
         I returned to the ritual,
waxing once a month, and it took me six years to rebel.
I switched to cream, a less utilitarian means.
      The results were disastrous: It smelled
         destructive, demanded more treatments,
caused pink eruptions near my mouth, uglier than the hair.
I tried a second brand, two creams: one opaque, scented
      rose for removal,
         the other clear, an after-cream
to soothe the skin, prevent pimples. It did not work at all.
I had tampered with the nature of my face. I yearned
      to be fresh-faced, windblown, organic
         or even hairy. I let it grow.
My inheritance re-emerged black and stiffer. I
struggled to find it beautiful for myself and my heirs,
      ignored my penchant
         to see my image as bristling,
rejoiced secretly when the summer sun turned me blonder
and my moustache invisible, and hoped for a flash,
      a permanent paling, an end to
         bouts with demons whose hairy fingers

would never quit my face and allow even two inches
of blonde lip. October came and diluted my tan.
      In November my
            blonde hairs vanished. December brought
back the brunette. I wanted peace and no hair. I settled
for compromise. I perform new rites of whitening:
      On a minute white tray, I blend one
           part "accelerating" powder with
two parts "greaseless" white cream, making sure that I am thorough.
Then, carefully, with a tiny white spoon (both these tools
      come in the bleach box),
      I spread the paste around my lips,
let it dry twelve minutes (no cooking, no pain, no mess) while
it surreptitiously softens and whitens, lightens,
      even brightens the surfacing
           memory, my mother's moustache.

Placemats

Fanny Hanna Moore, 1886-1980

When I iron them, the embroidery
stays damp. A pink sloop approaches or leaves
an umber pier. You did needle-
point – an Aesop rug – but these caught your eye
some trip south of the border, a color-
fast memory that's outlived you. Vase shaped

like a pineapple, fountain whose spray shapes
a willow: It's all embroidery,
this veranda you've left, a few colors
to seem what they become. Dark and lime leaves
dazzle gray georgette. Your designing eye
leapt at those two greens, at needle

skill that stitched musicians, balcony; needles
that laid in outline, stitched satiny shapes,
a drooping frond, a balustrade. By eye
or pattern? I don't do embroidery,
I iron it – lamp, bungalow, leaves
a green corona for one bloom your color

lavender. It's the herb not the color
you crush in my palm – aromatic, needle-
new. You pick a lamb's ear, touch flannel leaves
to my six-year-old cheek. You were shaping
my senses. A church, mauve spires embroidered
to grip a gray sky: Your death day, my eye

made the church of child Sundays small. My eyes
remember size less well than color,
but memory, unlike embroidery,
can't stitch away regret. It needles
me that when you lost speech, mouth shaping
just mumbles, I never touched lamb's ear leaves

to your pearl-pink, freckled cheek. Apple leaves
parasol your purple sofa swing. Eyes
on you, my mouth exaggerating word shapes,
I'd hold your hand, wishing language were color,
something to be stitched with a needle,
chamber music. If I were to embroider

the truth, I'd say I didn't leave when color
drained from your hair, when your eyes lost needle
spark, your mouth the will to shape embroidery.

Memoir

for J.J. Mitchell, dead of AIDS 4/26/86

I first remember you in Paris, blaze
of a smile, eleven years ago. Today
Joan tells me you're dead, the first I've loved
dead of that disease. It was New Year's Eve.
We sat on St. Germain drinking, watching
a boy in a convict black and white striped
Edwardian bathing suit weave festive
traffic on a skateboard – you, wild with
talk and blond hair. We had run into you
and Joe, and with you we walked to a dark
turreted flat on Ile St. Louis to meet
the silent, pale boy who was your lover.

I would not have said love then, didn't know
as we drank I watched your face to learn
what ignited your laugh: How might I live
to come to that? You lived outside Paris,
in a forest, you said, at an old mill
with a famous woman painter. My mother
had died. The man I loved bored me. You had
drugs and you were homosexual. I
wouldn't have said I too had drugs, was
in my wine where you were in whatever
one drinks with a famous woman at the end
of her looks, or smokes with a quiet boy.

"He killed himself," you said, smoking on the street
years later in New York. I didn't say
I had become homosexual, and you
didn't say the boy's death had caused you much

aside from anger. But you got sober. Paul
said so Christmas Eve before he left us
to cook what he would serve at your bed.
And I got sober. Today when Joan
told me of your death, we both said, "but he was
in recovery." The young woman who
drank with you amazed at a boy on a skate
New Year's Eve never saw you grin sober,

but I have the image of Paul at St. Mark's
days after your death, waving. I didn't
know what I was learning in how he lifted
his hand, but I have what the loss meant:
how his hat hid his eyes, how blond winter
grass hides a blue pond as I stop my car now
to speak a prayer for the dead. "Sober you can
do anything," you told Joan. Jimmy said
your last days the virus at your brain had you
in summer at the door on Fire Island
offering refreshments as guests arrived,
beautiful men, one after another.

Notes

In Mrs. N's Palace. Italicized words are titles of Nevelson sculpture.

Poem for the End. I have used, with permission of the translator, variations of the line "Did you think love was just a chat at a small table?" from "Poem of the End" by Marina Tsvetaeva, translated by Paul Schmidt.

Cleis. Italicized lines are from *Sappho: A New Translation* by Mary Barnard, Berkeley and Los Angeles, 1958.

Honor Moore was born in New York City in 1945. She grew up in Jersey City, New Jersey and Indianapolis, Indiana. *Mourning Pictures*, a verse play produced on Broadway in 1974, won her a CAPS grant from the New York State Council on the Arts and is anthologized in *The New Women's Theatre: Ten Plays by Contemporary American Women* which she edited. In 1981 she received a National Endowment Fellowship in poetry. Honor Moore now lives in rural Connecticut where she is at work on a biography of her grandmother, the painter Margarett Sargent.

Order form

Chicory Blue Press
795 East Street North
Goshen, CT 06756
(203) 491-2271

Please send me _____ copies of *Memoir* at $11.95 each.
$10.95 each if ordered before December 1988.

please print
Name _____

Address _____

_____

Connecticut residents: Please add 7 $1/2$% sales tax.

Shipping: $1.00 for the first book and 35 cents for each
additional book. For Air Mail: $2.50 per book.

Also available from Chicory Blue Press at $14.95 each:
A Wider Giving: Women Writing after a Long Silence, edited by
Sondra Zeidenstein. Poetry and prose by women who made
their major commitment to writing *after the age of forty-five*.
Includes autobiographical narratives by each writer.
"A masterly achievement." *May Sarton*